What's Inside My Body?

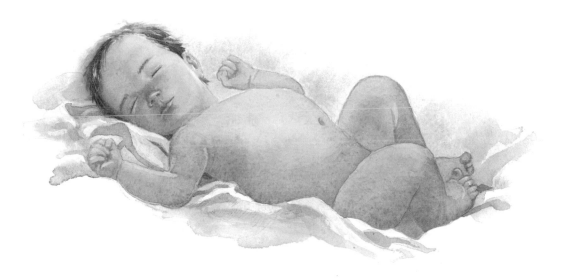

by
Lisa McCourt &
Lisa M. Bernstein
illustrated by Pat Grant Porter

ROXBURY PARK

LOWELL HOUSE JUVENILE
LOS ANGELES
NTC/Contemporary Publishing Group

**FOR
CULLEN WELSH
AND
KATHLEEN CANNON
—L.M.**

**FOR
JESSICA HAYS
—P.G.P.**

**FOR
DAIVA LEE PLISCOU
AND
WILSON NORMAN PLISCOU
—L.M.B.**

Published by Lowell House
A division of NTC/Contemporary Publishing Group, Inc.
4255 West Touhy Avenue, Lincolnwood (Chicago), Illinois 60712-1975 U.S.A.

Lowell House books can be purchased at special discounts when ordered in bulk for premiums and special sales. Contact Department CS at the following address:
NTC/Contemporary Publishing Group
4255 West Touhy Avenue
Lincolnwood, IL 60712-1975
1-800-323-4900

ISBN: 0-7373-0463-4
Library of Congress Control Number: 00-133224

Roxbury Park is a division of NTC/Contemporary Publishing Group, Inc.

Managing Director and Publisher: Jack Artenstein
Editor in Chief, Roxbury Park Books: Michael Artenstein
Director of Publishing Services: Rena Copperman
Director of Art Production: Bret Perry
Senior Editor: Maria Magallanes
Editorial Assistant: Nicole Monastirsky

Printed and bound in Singapore
00 01 02 TWP 10 9 8 7 6 5 4 3 2 1

Contents

Introduction

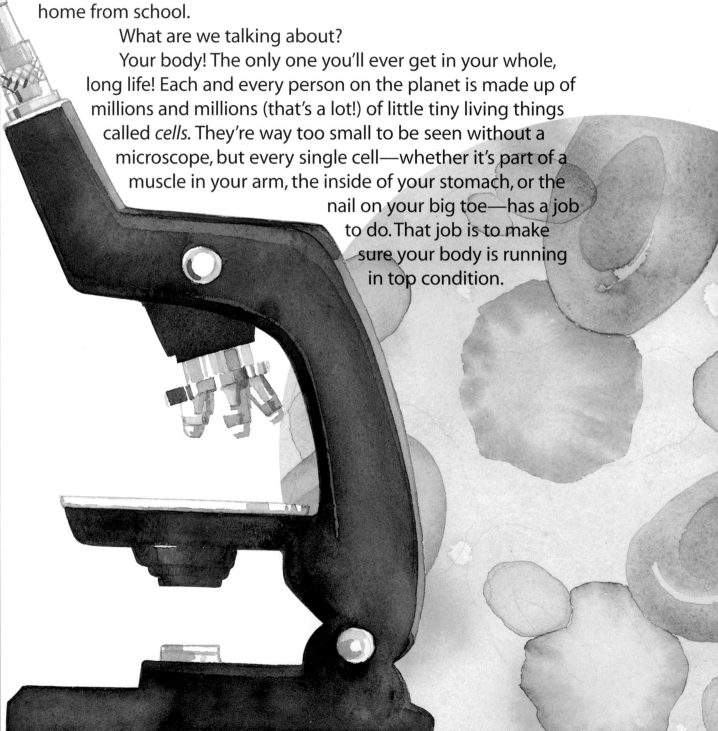

You can feed it. You can clean it. You can bump it, bruise it, twist it into funny shapes, and roll it down a hill. Because of it, you can walk, talk, eat, sleep, play soccer, run a race, swim, dance, read a book, and watch a movie.

But you can't trade it in for a new one, or lose it on the way home from school.

What are we talking about?

Your body! The only one you'll ever get in your whole, long life! Each and every person on the planet is made up of millions and millions (that's a lot!) of little tiny living things called *cells*. They're way too small to be seen without a microscope, but every single cell—whether it's part of a muscle in your arm, the inside of your stomach, or the nail on your big toe—has a job to do. That job is to make sure your body is running in top condition.

And even though everybody's cells are alike, no one else in the entire world has a body just like yours. Not your brother or your sister (no matter how much your Aunt Elaine says you look alike), or even your identical twin. You are absolutely, totally, 100% unique.

And just think, all this happened without any effort on your part! You were born with everything you needed to survive, to grow, and to learn—all parts included.

So, what makes this amazing body of yours work? What are the different pieces that make it go? And what's all that stuff inside it, anyway? Let's go in for a look!

Your Brain

The big star of the show is that wrinkly blob of matter under your baseball cap. Well, under your hair. Actually, it's inside your head. Weighing in at a mere 3 pounds (and made up of more than 75% water), your brain is the master of your own personal universe. It's better, faster, and smarter than any computer ever invented. It sends and receives billions of messages a day—taking in all kinds of information about what's going on both inside you and outside you, and at the same time telling your body what to do, how to do it, and when to do it. It's also in charge of thoughts ("It's time to feed the dog"), feelings ("Gosh! I'm really happy right now!"), memory ("Oh yeah! I put my sneakers under the bed!"), and learning ("The capital of Idaho is Boise").

In fact, your brain is so efficient at taking care of you that you might not even realize just how much it does. For example, ever thought about how many motions you go through just to get up from a chair and walk across a room? A lot! But all you really have to do is think, "There's the doorbell! I'd better go see who it is!" And the next thing you know, you're up, moving, and at the door. You didn't have to tell yourself, "Okay, now I need to bend my legs, stand up, make sure I don't lose my balance ... Now I move first my right foot, now my left foot—oops, I'd better not forget to swing my arms ... Hey, eyeballs—keep looking at the door! Now it's time to move my right foot again, and now my left one ..." Get the point?

Your clever brain has taken charge, leaving you with only the job of wondering who it is outside your house.

But as important as the brain is to everything you do, it doesn't work all by itself. It's like a railroad conductor, and all those messages it sends and receives are like tiny railroad cars, zooming all over your body. Those railroad cars need a track to travel on—that track is called your *nervous system*.

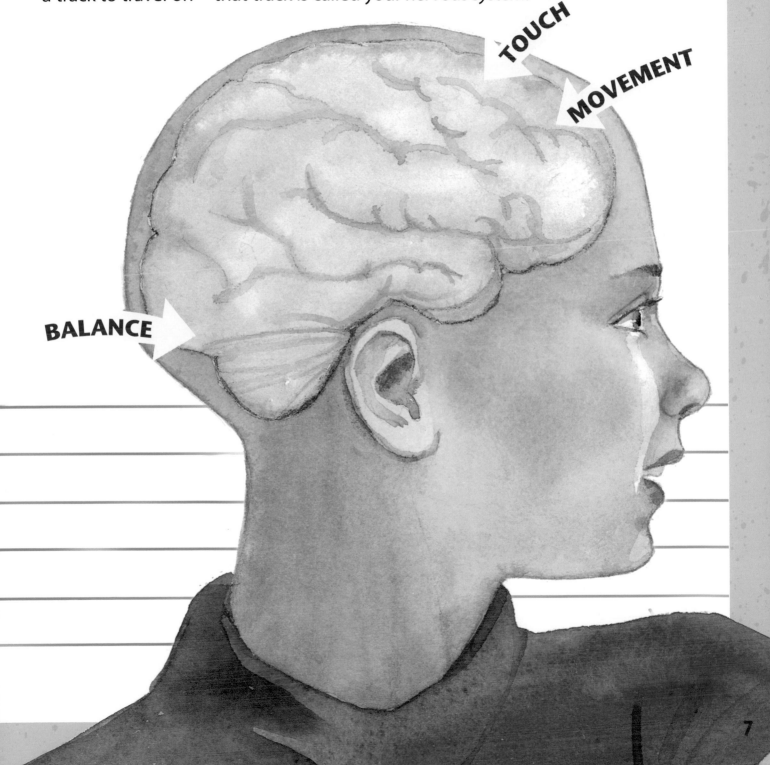

Your Nervous System

Welcome to your nervous system, a 50-mile-long network of nerves! (Nerves are just long bunches of nerve cells grouped together.) These nerve cells send and receive signals from the brain—just like those railroad cars zipping around on their tracks.

The nervous system is made up of three parts. The *central nervous system* is the first part, and it's really, really busy carrying all those messages between the brain and your body. It's made up of your brain and your spinal cord, which is—guess where?—in your spine.

The second part, the *peripheral nervous system*, is linked to the central nervous system by a bunch of nerves that weave throughout your body and end at points all over your skin. The areas of your skin that have the most nerve endings are the most sensitive to touch. (These include your fingertips and—pucker up!—your lips.)

The third part of your nervous system is called the *autonomous nervous system*. That's the part that tells your heart to beat, your lungs to breathe, and your guts to digest food. It's all done for you automatically.

So you never have to say, "Omigosh, I forgot to breathe this morning!" (You'll learn more about your heart, your lungs, and your digestive system later on in the book, so stay tuned!)

central
nervous system

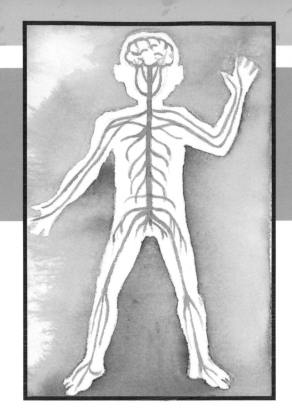

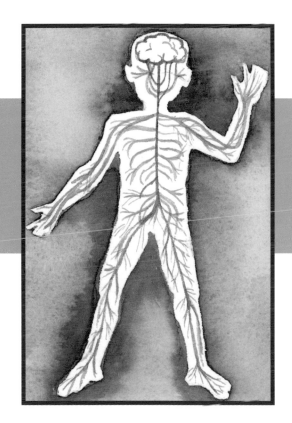

peripheral
nervous system

autonomous
nervous system

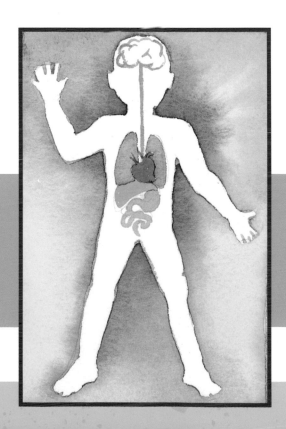

Your Eyes and Sense of Sight

From the second you wake up in the morning until you go to sleep at night, your eyes are on the job, keeping you informed about the size, shape, color, and location of everything around you.

These amazing organs are two little balls of fluid, each with a clear window (the *cornea*) in the front. Light rays pass through the eye and onto a wall at the back of the eye (the *retina*), kind of like a film being projected onto a movie screen. Only the light rays are bent so that everything your eye takes in at that point is actually upside down!

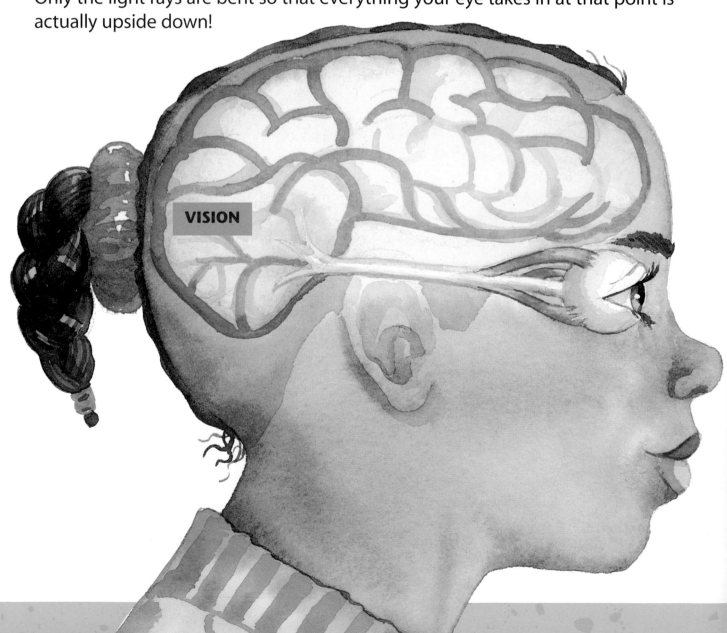

VISION

So how come you don't see everyone around you standing on their heads? Once again, your brain—linked by nerves to the eyes—comes to the rescue, and neatly turns everything right side up again, so that what you see . . . is what you get.

What color are your eyes? Green? Blue? Brown? Black? The color of your eyes comes from the amount of *pigment* (it's sort of like the body's version of paint) in your body. The more pigment you have, the darker your eyes are.

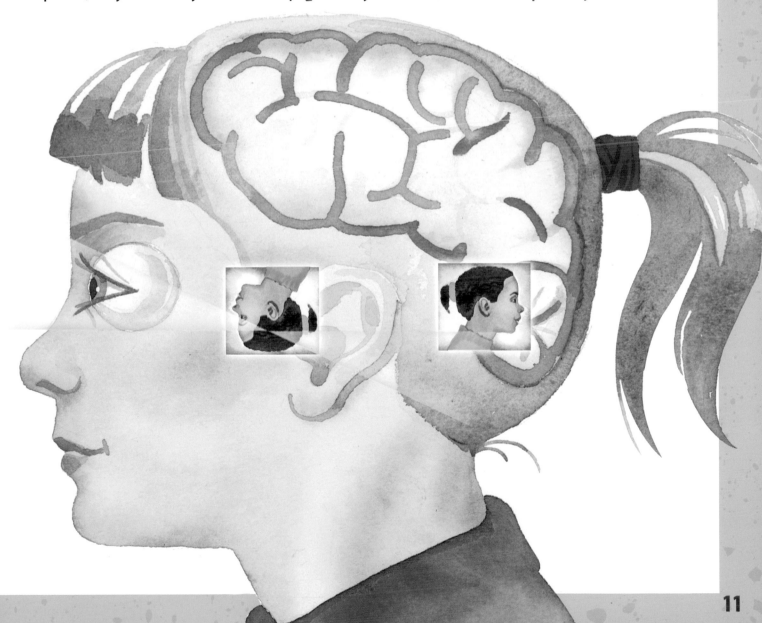

Your Ears and Sense of Hearing

Say what? Your ears let you hear the hundreds of sounds that fill your world every day: people talking, birds chirping, music playing, cars chugging down the street, to name just a few. But did you know that your ears help keep you balanced, too?

The human ear has three main parts. The first part, the *outer ear,* starts with that funny flap of stiff but flexible skin on the outside, and goes inside the ear to your eardrum. When sound waves hit the eardrum, it vibrates, just like the drum in a rock band vibrates when the drummer hits it with his sticks.

The second part, the *middle ear,* has three little linked bones (the *hammer,* the *anvil,* and the *stirrup*) that pick up sound waves and carry them along.

Inside the third part, the *inner ear,* is the *cochlea* (it looks like the coiled-up shell of a snail), which is the final stop for those sound waves.

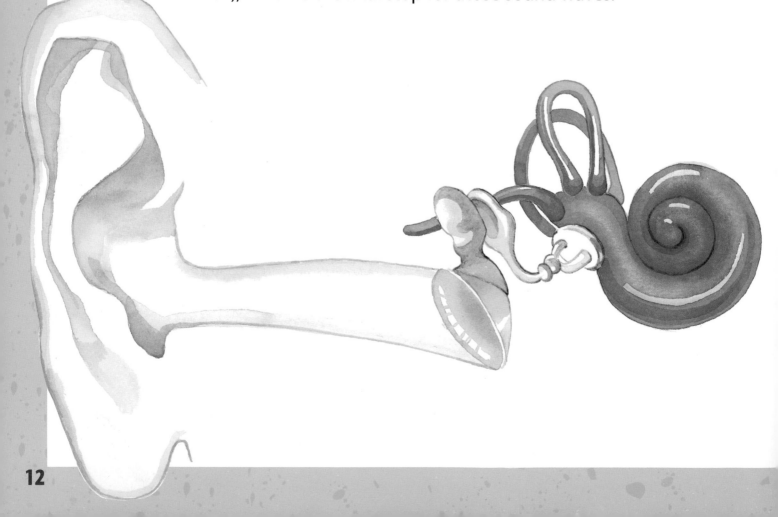

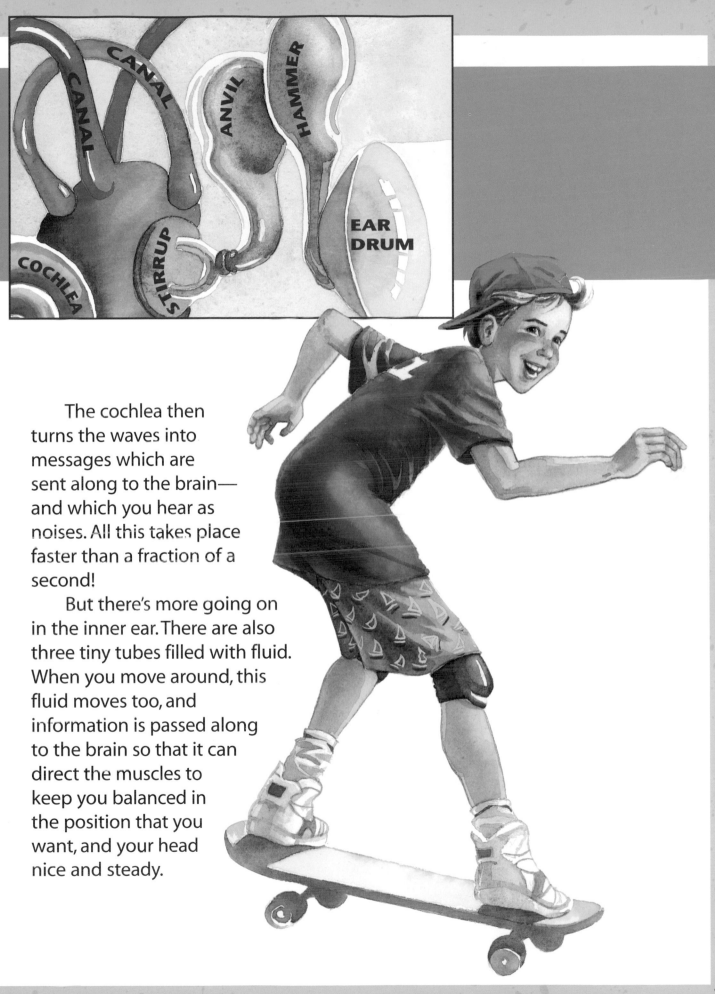

CANAL

CANAL

CANAL

ANVIL

HAMMER

STIRRUP

COCHLEA

EAR DRUM

The cochlea then turns the waves into messages which are sent along to the brain—and which you hear as noises. All this takes place faster than a fraction of a second!

But there's more going on in the inner ear. There are also three tiny tubes filled with fluid. When you move around, this fluid moves too, and information is passed along to the brain so that it can direct the muscles to keep you balanced in the position that you want, and your head nice and steady.

Your Nose and Sense of Smell

As any nose knows, there's a *big* difference between the scent of a freshly picked flower and the tuna-fish sandwich you forgot to take out of your lunch sack three days ago. How can you tell the difference? That's the job of a whole bunch of *sensors* (a fancy term for a thing that senses or detects something) inside your nose. Each of these sensors, called a *receptor,* has tiny hairs covered with sticky mucus (bet you didn't know that snot actually helps you to smell things!) to help "trap" a scent. Then the receptors can send messages along to your brain, which figures out exactly what each odor is.

And snot does more than that! It's got a special chemical in it that coats those tiny hairs inside your nose and kills bacteria. When your nose sucks up air that's dirty with smoke, pollen, dust, and other yucky things, the snot-covered hairs try to keep those things from getting into your body.

When enough dirt gets stuck in the sticky snot, it forms the crusty little clumps we call boogers. The more you breathe after a booger has formed, the more dried out it will get. So your wet boogers are still young, and your dry, hard boogers are the ones that have been hanging around for a while.

Your nose makes new snot about every twenty minutes. But it doesn't stay in your nose. Without even realizing it, you swallow almost a quart of it every day! Unless you blow the dirt-filled snot out of your nose (into a tissue, please!), it goes down your throat and into your stomach where, thank goodness, it is quickly processed and disposed of.

Your Tongue and Sense of Taste

Mmmm! An icy-cold chocolate ice cream cone . . . Mom's meat loaf . . . French fries . . . Cookies right out of the oven! Is your mouth watering yet? Then say thanks to your amazing tongue, because without it, everything you eat would taste exactly the same. And that would get pretty boring, pretty fast.

Luckily for us, the human tongue is loaded with almost 9,000 little tiny receptor cells—better known as taste buds—which send information along to the brain about what it is your fork has just slid into your mouth. Then it's up to your brain to decide whether you like it (sirloin steak) or not (brussels sprouts, anyone?).

Our taste buds can classify tastes into four major categories: sour (like a lemon), salty (what you sprinkle on those fries), bitter (like coffee and certain greens), and sweet (most any kind of dessert!). All of the foods and liquids we eat and drink fit somewhere into these four groups.

And here's something else to chew on: ever notice how food seems to lose its flavor when you have a cold? That's because the sense of taste is closely linked to the sense of smell—so when your nose is stuffed up, the slice of "everything" pizza that just landed on your plate probably won't smell or taste as good as it usually does!

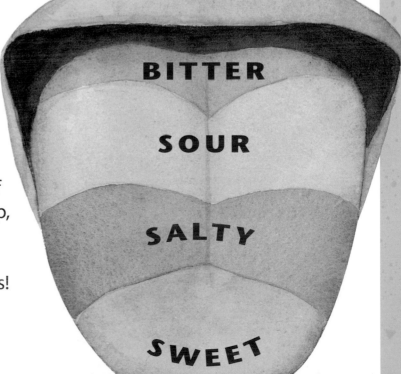

BITTER

SOUR

SALTY

SWEET

Your Skin and Sense of Touch

Quick! Name the biggest organ in your body!

If you said "the heart" or "the stomach," you're wrong—believe it or not, it's your skin. Weighing in at a hefty 8 pounds, skin covers the entire surface of your body and does a terrific job of protecting you from the environment (it's waterproof, and plus it keeps out germs). It also helps to keep your temperature constant. You sweat when you're too hot, and as the sweat dries up, the body cools down. When you're too cold, you get goose bumps—which are really itty-bitty muscles in your skin that rise up, trying to trap a warm layer of air next to your body.

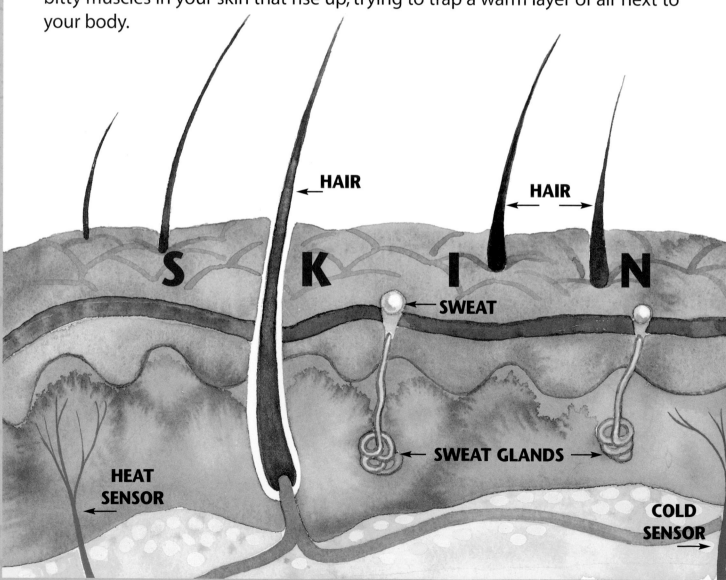

HAIR

HAIR

S K I N

SWEAT

SWEAT GLANDS

HEAT SENSOR

COLD SENSOR

And, of course, the skin is what helps you to *feel* the world around you, allowing you to sense warmth, cold, pain, pressure, and any kind of touch.

Remember when you read about the peripheral nervous system? It's the receptors in your skin, linked to your nervous system and your brain, which bring alive the world of feeling, from "Hey, it's freezing outside!" to "Ouch! That cocoa is too hot!" to "Oh, this bath is just right."

Your skin is also responsible for something else you probably never thought of: dust. A whopping 90% of the dust in your house is made up of dead skin cells! Think about *that* the next time you run your finger across your dusty knick-knack shelf!

Your Bones

If you ever heard a little kid say, "I have more bones than *you* do!" you'd probably think the kid was nuts. But he might be right! Babies are born with over 300 bones, but as they grow, some of the bones fuse together so that adults only have about 206. Even among grown-ups, the number of bones can vary since some people have more bones in their hands and their feet (where *half* of all the bones are!) than others do.

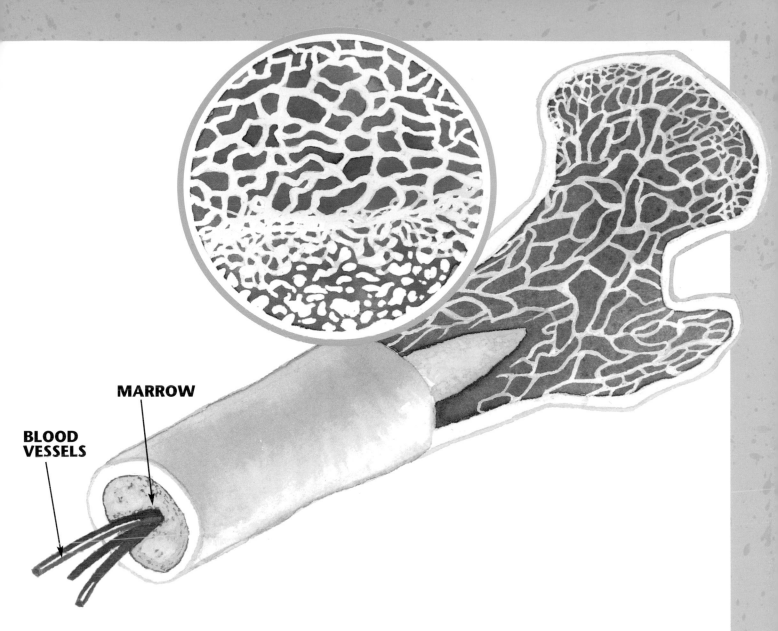

MARROW

BLOOD VESSELS

Strong and sturdy, your bones perform the important job of holding your body together and helping to protect the stuff inside. If you've ever seen a picture of a skeleton at Halloween, you've got a pretty good idea of what most of your bones look like. And if you've ever looked at real bones—like in a museum—you might have guessed that your own bones are just hard, dry, funny-shaped things (like driftwood on a beach). Not so! The bones in your body are made up of living, growing cells. That's why most broken bones are able to heal quickly by themselves. And the fact that bones are alive helps in another way to keep you healthy, too. Inside many bones is a soft, fatty substance called *marrow,* which makes the new blood cells your body needs to keep you healthy. (You'll learn more about the importance of blood cells later.)

Your Muscles and Joints

Bones are important, but without muscles and joints to help them along, they'd be going nowhere! The places where the bones meet are called *joints,* and they're held together by *ligaments* and *tendons,* which are tough, stretchy things (think of the elastic on a brand-new pair of socks).

Okay, now that the skeleton is all connected by joints, ligaments, and tendons, how do we get the body to move? With *muscles,* of course! Muscles look like long rows of tubes or cables all stacked together. These cables are made up of lots and lots of special long cells. Did you know that muscles account for almost half of your entire body weight?

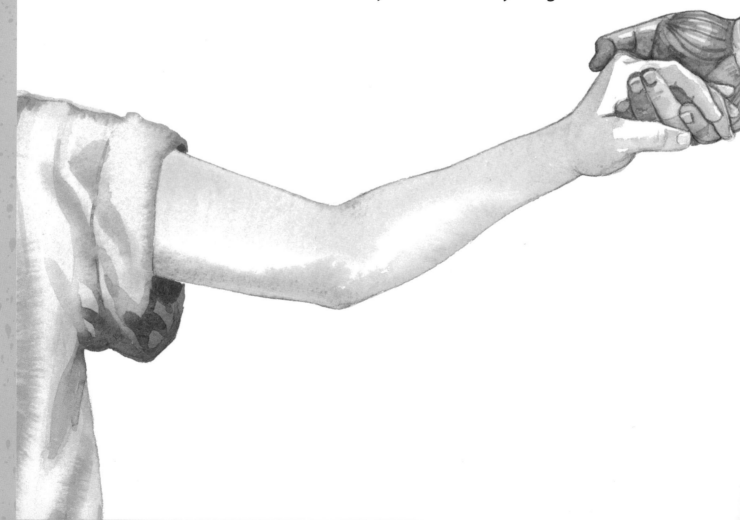

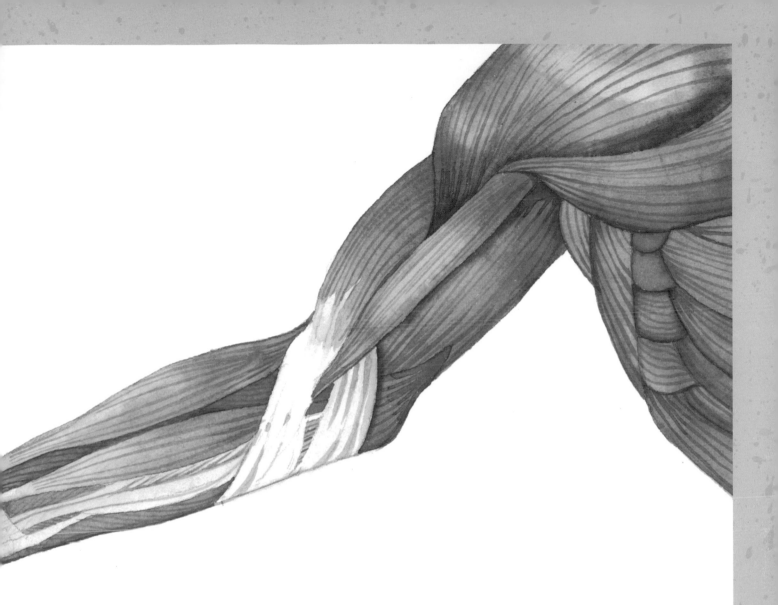

Muscles are attached to the bones so that they can pull (but never push!) those bones around at your command. Every time you kick a ball, scratch your head, or pet your cat, your brain sends a message to the muscles that control those parts of your body. ("Hey, muscles! Move that arm bone so the kid can scratch his head!") You've got over 600 muscles in all—and in the simple act of walking you use over 200 of 'em!

Want to guess where your strongest muscles are? If you said they're in your arm or your leg, you're wrong. The very strongest muscles in your whole body are in your mouth—the ones that let you bite things. And your busiest muscles? They're the ones that move your eyeballs around!

Your Heart, Blood, and Circulatory System

Ever gotten a cut, seen that bright red stuff oozing from your skin, and wondered what blood is all about? You might be surprised to know that blood is made up of more than 50% plain old water! The rest is tiny little cells—there are three kinds. First are the *red blood cells,* which transport oxygen. (There's more on oxygen soon.) Next are the *white blood cells,* which are like little soldiers, helping your body fight off sickness and disease. And finally there are the *platelets,* which are the cells that stop that cut of yours from bleeding so that it can start to heal.

WHITE CELL

GERM

PLATELETS

RED CELL

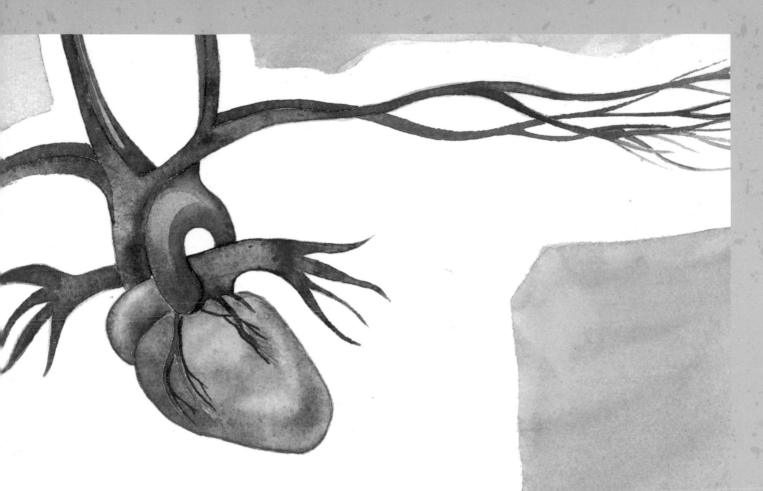

And how does all your blood—about 9 pints of it in the average person—get around your body? It's moved by that powerhouse muscle located in the middle of your chest, the heart! Only about the size of a clenched fist, your heart pumps all the time—night and day, around the clock, 100,000 times every 24 hours. Its job is to keep blood flowing throughout your body in special little tubes called arteries, capillaries, and veins.

Arteries take the blood away from your heart. *Capillaries* take energy from the food you eat and oxygen from the air you breathe to your body's cells. Finally, *veins* carry away the waste from the cells and bring the blood back to your heart. And then the whole process starts all over again. It's because of this awesome delivery system— some 60 miles of blood vessels—that your body stays energized and functioning!

Your Lungs and Breathing

You've already read about how you need energy from food and from oxygen in the air. But how exactly does the body turn these things into energy? It takes two of the body's systems, working together, to make that happen.

The first system is the *digestive system,* which has to do with eating, digesting, and pooping. The food you eat is broken down and sent into your bloodstream. The blood takes it to the cells, remember?

But the cells also need oxygen in order to get energy from your food, and that's where the second system comes in: the *respiratory system,* which has to do with breathing.

Your lungs—a pair of big flexible sacs positioned on either side of your heart—make up the respiratory system, along with your nose, your mouth, and your *trachea,* or windpipe. Every time you breathe, oxygen enters your body. (Oxygen is part of the air around us, and it's one thing human beings can't live without.) It goes down your windpipe and into your lungs, where the oxygen combines with red blood cells and is then carried to all the parts of your body.

When the oxygen meets up with the broken-down food, energy is released. This energy lets your lungs breathe, your heart pump, your brain work, and it allows your body to do the hundreds of jobs it needs to do to keep you alive and well.

When energy is released, waste is created, too. Our bodies produce different kinds of waste. One, carbon dioxide (it's an invisible gas, like oxygen), is carried away by the blood and is automatically disposed of every time you exhale, or breathe out. Another kind of waste is also carried away by the blood. It eventually becomes poop and pee-pee (or *feces* and *urine,* if that's what your mother makes you say). You'll learn more about *that* interesting stuff later in this book.

Your Kidneys, Liver, and Pancreas

Everyone can't be a star—you need behind-the-scenes people to keep any play or movie going. And that's also the role of three quiet, but very important, organs located in your midsection: the kidneys (you've got two of them), the liver, and the pancreas. They may not get as much attention as your brain or your heart do, but they also have big jobs to take care of!

The *kidneys* (yes, they look just like those beans floating around in minestrone soup) are located just beneath your stomach. They're part of your body's waste-disposal system. Every last drop of your blood flows through your kidneys 40 times a day so your kidneys can separate out all the stuff your body doesn't need anymore, and convert it into the waste product known as urine.

Your *liver* is the body's largest *internal* organ, weighing about 3 pounds. Located just beneath your lungs, it's super-busy, performing over 500 different tasks within the body! Its most important jobs? Helping with digestion is one. Another is to cleanse the blood—it's so good at it, in fact, that an amazing 25% of your blood flows through your liver every minute.

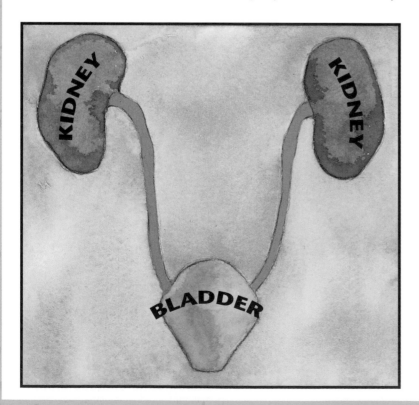

The *pancreas* is another organ tucked in close to your stomach, and for a good reason, too. Its main job is to help with digestion. It creates 1½ quarts of digestive juice a day to help break down the foods you eat into smaller and smaller particles that your body can convert into the energy it needs to keep going.

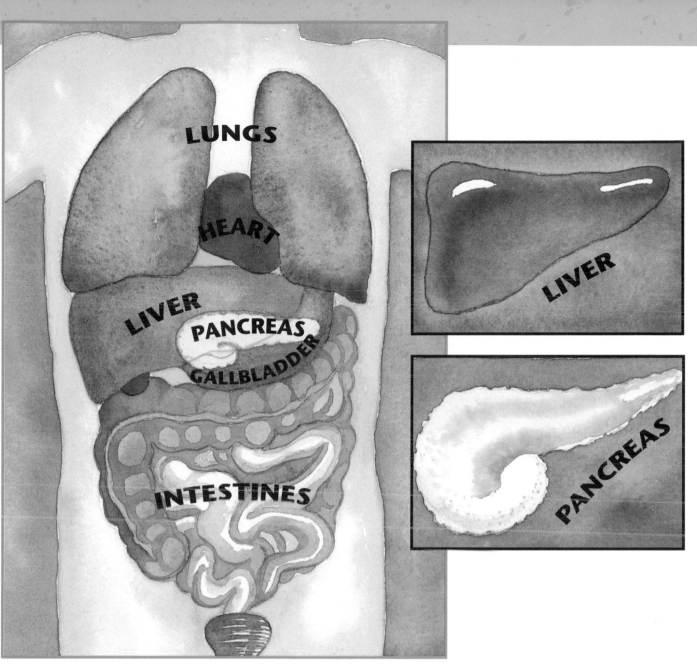

LUNGS

HEART

LIVER

PANCREAS

GALLBLADDER

INTESTINES

LIVER

PANCREAS

DIGESTIVE JUICE

ONE QUART

DIGESTIVE JUICE

ONE QUART

DIGESTIVE JUICE

ONE QUART

Your Teeth

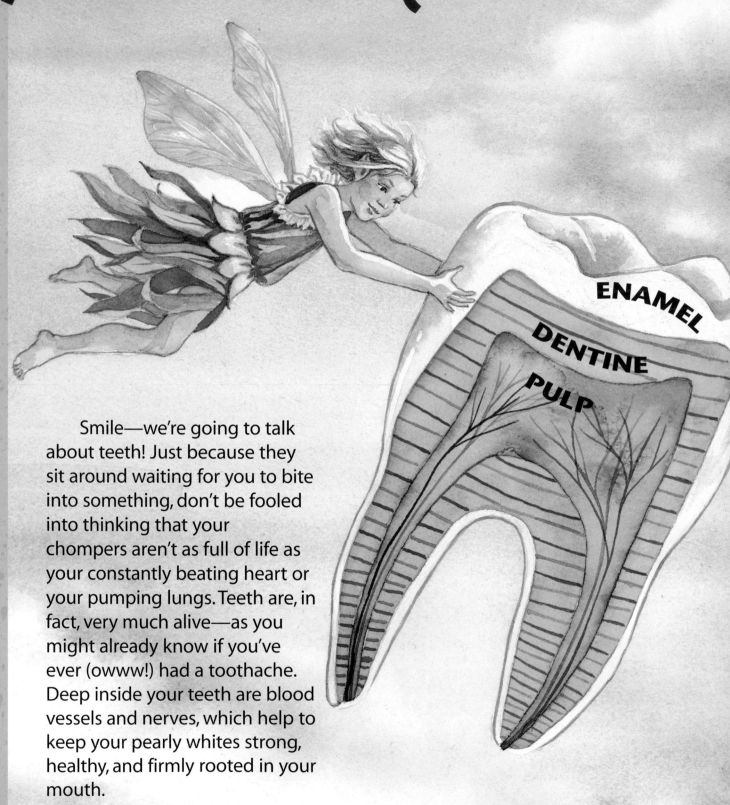

ENAMEL

DENTINE

PULP

Smile—we're going to talk about teeth! Just because they sit around waiting for you to bite into something, don't be fooled into thinking that your chompers aren't as full of life as your constantly beating heart or your pumping lungs. Teeth are, in fact, very much alive—as you might already know if you've ever (owww!) had a toothache. Deep inside your teeth are blood vessels and nerves, which help to keep your pearly whites strong, healthy, and firmly rooted in your mouth.

When you were born you probably didn't have any teeth (so you looked kind of funny when you grinned), but before your first birthday your teeth started to poke their way out into your gums. A six-year-old has about 20 baby, or milk, teeth which get replaced with permanent teeth. A grown-up has a total of 32 teeth.

A tooth has three main parts. The outer part is made up of tough stuff called *enamel* and is the hardest substance in the human body. This is the part that you brush and floss (every night, right?). Underneath the enamel is *dentine,* which is hard, but not as hard. And finally, there's the *pulp cavity* ("cavity" is another word for "hole"), which is where the nerves and blood vessels are located.

Teeth help us to speak clearly and give shape to our faces, but their most important job is to chew our food, getting us started on that long and interesting process called *digestion.* So do you want to know more about what happens after you've popped that tasty handful of popcorn into your mouth? Turn the page!

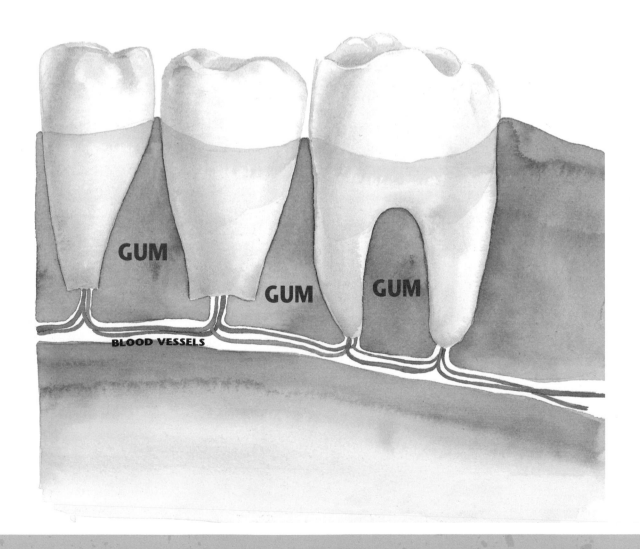

GUM

GUM   GUM

BLOOD VESSELS

Digestion
Part 1: Your Mouth, Stomach, and Small Intestine

Digestion begins the second you put any kind of food into your mouth and start chewing. That watery stuff that keeps your mouth wet (its fancy name is *saliva* but you probably call it spit) starts to break down food right away. Spit is 99.5% water, but it also contains mucus (the part that makes spit slimy), plus some chemicals called *enzymes* (the stuff that breaks down the food) and even—brace yourself—tiny bits of urine. Try telling your friends that they have pee-pee in their mouths. They won't believe you, but it's true! The pee-pee comes along with the spit produced by several special organs, called *glands,* lining the insides of your cheeks. Now, please don't think badly of your spit! It is actually a very cool substance. It kills bacteria, makes your food easier to chew, and without it how could you ever spit watermelon seeds across the room?

Okay. You've chewed your food, you've swallowed it, and down it goes along an 8-inch-long tube called the *esophagus*. Then it arrives in the stomach—a big flexible bag of muscles—and the real destruction begins! Those muscles get to work, and enzymes, along with strong acids, do a number on that burger you just gobbled. It can take between three and six hours for the stomach to do its work, until finally all that's left of your lunch is a thick, nicely churned liquid called *chyme* (rhymes with "rhyme!")

Next that chyme travels to your small intestine (which is actually a whopping 16 feet long). Strong muscles, along with digestive juices from your liver and pancreas, keep the chyme moving along. Meanwhile, all the nutrients pass right through the small intestine and into your bloodstream so your body can use it. This part of the digestive process can take between four and six hours.

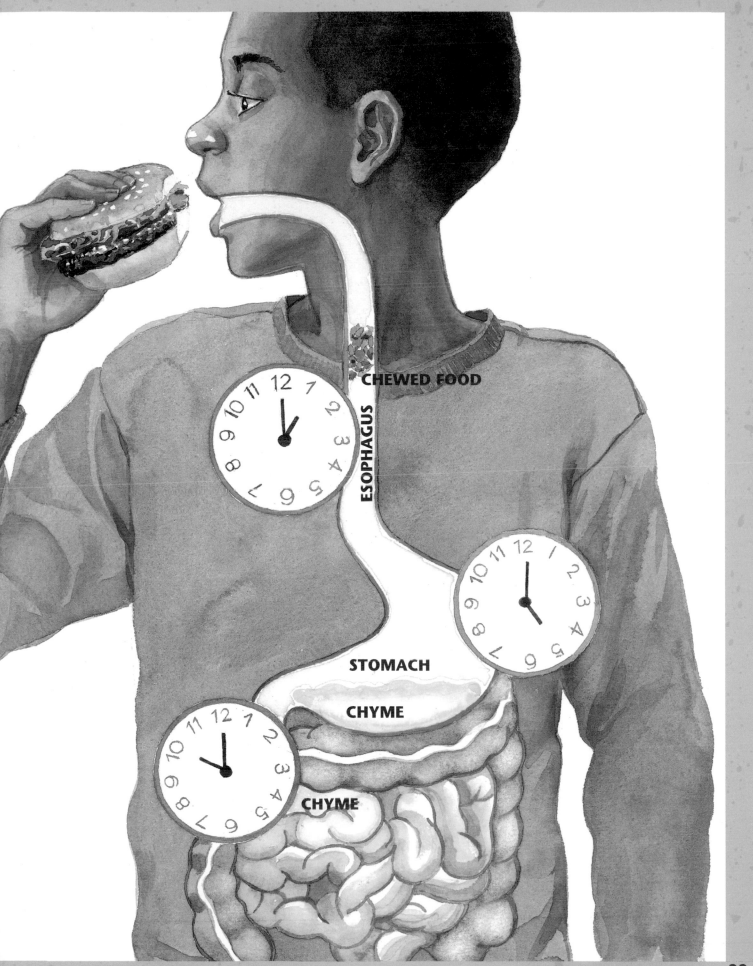

CHEWED FOOD

ESOPHAGUS

STOMACH

CHYME

CHYME

Digestion
Part 2: Your Large Intestine, Poop, and Pee

So what's left of the chyme now that the small intestine is through with it? It becomes a waste product, and is sent along to your large intestine, which is about 5 feet long. Here most of the water is absorbed, and the waste continues to a 5-inch-long tube in your bottom called the *rectum*. When your body is finally done processing everything, muscles in the rectum squeeze out that waste—better known as poop.

Help! My poop is alive! No, it's not a line from a really gross horror movie. It's the truth. About half of what makes up your poop is living bacteria. (But don't worry, your poop isn't about to start doing the backstroke across your toilet.) Bacteria—little tiny creatures so small you can't even see them— live inside your intestines and do the important job of gobbling up whatever food hasn't been absorbed into your bloodstream. They're the reason your poop smells the way it does. They make gasses (remember when we talked about car exhaust?) that leave your body as farts.

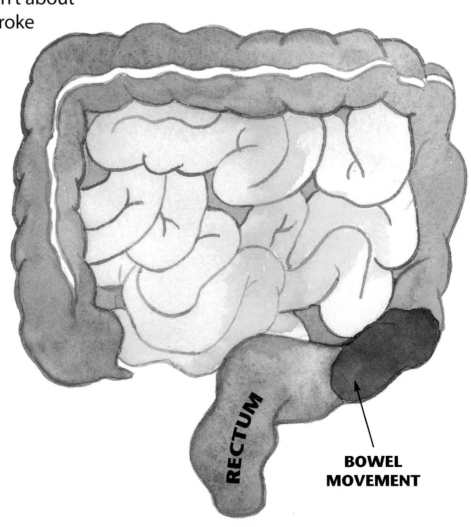

RECTUM

BOWEL MOVEMENT

Now, you might have wondered why poop is always pretty much that same dark-brown color, when you start off the digestive process by eating foods that are lots of different colors. Let's say that you ate an orange, spaghetti with tomato sauce and meatballs, potato chips, creamed spinach, and a vanilla cupcake with pink icing. What happens to all those colors along that 30-foot-long journey from your mouth to your hiney? Well, your liver makes stuff called *bile,* which helps to digest the chyme as it moves along the intestines. Bile is made from old red blood cells your body doesn't need anymore, and it comes in shades of yellow, green, and brown. Those busy little bacteria break down the bile so that it ends up turning poop that familiar chocolate-brown color you know and love.

We can't end this section on digestion without talking about that other important waste product—urine. A lot of people think that pee-pee is just as gross as poop, but it's really a whole lot different. Peeing is just your body's way of getting rid of water it doesn't need. There's no bacteria in your pee-pee, so it's way cleaner than poop. Believe it or not, it's even cleaner than your spit and your skin! (At least when it first leaves your body—not when it's been sitting in the toilet for a while, so be sure and flush!) Pee is 96% water. The rest of it is stuff your body didn't need.

Digestion

Part 3: Puking and Diarrhea

More often than not, the digestive process goes pretty smoothly. You might have a few noisy tummy rumbles from time to time, or maybe have to fart when you really didn't want to (like in class), but all in all your body takes care of things pretty well.

Sometimes, though, those tummy rumbles turn into something else and all of a sudden your stomach is churning like someone turned on a blender down there. The next thing you know, up comes supper!

What makes your body vomit, or puke, anyway? You might be surprised to learn that your brain, not your belly, is in charge of issuing the upchuck orders. Inside your brain is a special place called the *vomit center,* which sends out the puke signal whenever anything bothers your stomach too much. Spoiled food, germs, viruses—even eating too much food that's perfectly okay can trigger the vomit center. Feeling off balance can cause some people's vomit centers to sound the alarm too, like when they ride a roller-coaster or go boating.

And what about on the other end of things? When your poop isn't nice, firm, and solid . . . but watery and runny, making you hurry to the bathroom a lot more than you want to? That's called *diarrhea,* and it can be caused by a whole lot of things—the flu, food allergies, drinking water from another country, being really upset (really!), and even certain medicines.

Whatever the cause is, your intestines react by moving things along too quickly, so that food particles don't always get broken down and water isn't absorbed as much as it usually is. The (tee hee) end result? There's a reason diarrhea's called "the runs"!

Your Hair and Nails

Is yours long? Short? Curly? Straight? Does it do funny things in damp weather? Your hair is one of the first things other people notice about you. And why not? You've got 100,000 strands of hair on your scalp alone!

You've got it all over your body, too. Amazingly, your skin is waterproof even though it's filled with thousands of teeny tiny holes. Some are pores, which let sweat through. And some are hair follicles ("follicle" is a fancy word for "hole"). Did you know that the shape of your follicles determines what kind of hair you have? If your hair follicles are round, you'll have straight hair. If your follicles are oval-shaped, your hair will be wavy. And if you have flat follicles, you'll have curly hair.

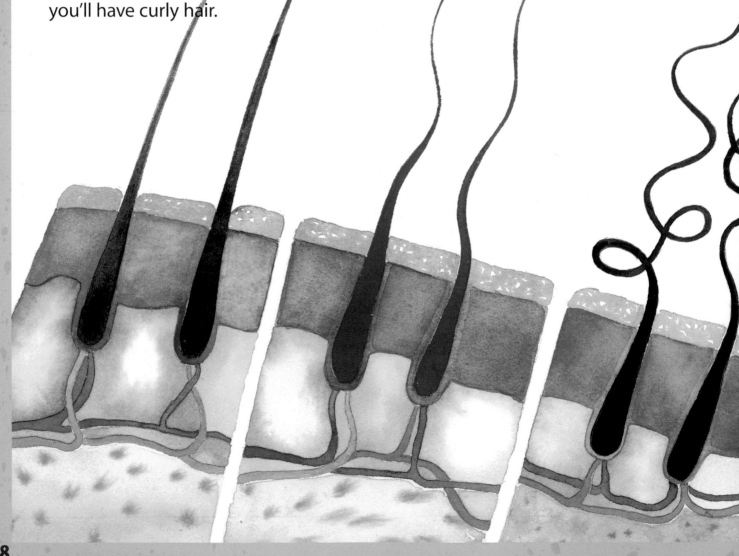

Hair, just like your fingernails and toenails, is made up of a tough substance called *keratin*. (It's the same stuff that the outer layer of your skin is made from.) If someone plucks one of your hairs, it's going to hurt a little bit. But when you get your hair cut, or your nails trimmed, you don't feel a thing. That's because your nails and hair don't have any nerves in them. There's nothing to send that painful "Ouch!" message to your brain.

Did you ever get a bad haircut? There's no use tugging at what you've got left to try and make it grow faster. Hair pretty much grows at a slow, steady rate of ½ inch a month. In the meantime, there's always a baseball cap!

Yawns and Hiccups, Laughter and Tears

Tired? Sleepy? Bored? You might just find yourself yawning. Believe it or not, scientists don't fully understand why we yawn. They know what happens when we do it—it brings in a fresh supply of oxygen to the lungs—but they can't explain the reason behind it. Or why, when we see other people yawning, we can't help but yawn ourselves. Just cover your mouth, please!

Hic! Hic! Hic! How'd you get that nasty case of hiccups, anyway? Maybe you ate or drank something too quickly. Then the nerves in your *diaphragm* (a muscle in your chest that sits between your lungs and your guts) got into the act, causing you to breathe in more quickly than usual. And *then* your windpipe tried to help, snapping shut so that too much air didn't come rushing in. Fortunately, hiccuping isn't serious, though it may be annoying. Try taking ten little sips of water from a glass, or swallowing a teaspoon of sugar. Everyone seems to have a "cure" for hiccups, but the good news is, sooner or later they'll go away on their own!

HIC

HIC

HIC

DIAPHRAGM

Did you just hear a good joke? You probably laughed. Among all the animals in nature (yes, human beings are animals, too!), we're the only ones who laugh. And we do it for different reasons. We laugh because we're happy. We laugh because something seems funny. We laugh because we're being tickled. And sometimes we even laugh because we're embarrassed. Whatever the reason, laughter involves the whole body. Did you know that a good belly laugh can cause 400 of your muscles to move? So go ahead and tell a joke, and laugh at it, too—it's good for you!

Ready for a sob story? The fact is, your eyes are making wet, salty tears all the time. It's a way of keeping your eyes nice and clean. But when you're sad ("My pet goldfish just died"), or frightened ("This movie is *scary!*"), or have very strong feelings about something ("I love you a lot, Teddy Bear"), you find yourself crying.

And it's best not to hold those tears back—scientists have found that crying can actually make you feel better. It's true! Hanky, anyone?

Your Reproductive System

BLADDER

TESTICLES

You already know that girls are different from boys. But how exactly do you know it? It's not because girls sometimes wear dresses, and boys don't. In places like Scotland and Africa, men wear outfits that look like skirts, and that's considered perfectly normal. And it's not because girls wear their hair longer than boys, either. You've probably seen lots of boys with long hair, and girls with really short hair!

One of the biggest differences between a girl and a boy has to do with what's *under* the clothing. The formal term is *reproductive system* (you might know it as "private parts"). This system has to do with how people, when they are grown up, reproduce—in other words, have babies. If we didn't have reproductive systems, we couldn't have babies, and before too long, there would be no more people! That's how important the reproductive system is!

The boy's reproductive system is easier to see, because it's mostly on the outside of his body. He has a *penis,* which he uses to go pee-pee, and which someday he'll use to put *sperm,* the stuff that helps to make a baby, inside a grown-up woman's body. At the base of his penis are two sacs, called *testicles.* That's where the sperm is made.

A girl's reproductive system is mostly on the inside of her body. Near her tummy she's got some curving tubes called *ovaries,* which have thousands of little tiny eggs inside them. Those eggs will someday travel along to a hollow, muscled place called her *uterus,* and if one of those eggs meets up with a sperm, a baby will be made! When that baby is ready, it will leave the woman's body through a flexible canal called a *vagina,* which is lined with skin that's a lot like the skin on the palm of your hands. Even though a girl's pee-pee seems to come out of her vagina, it's actually coming from a separate place—a little hole, called the *urethra,* which is located just above the vagina.

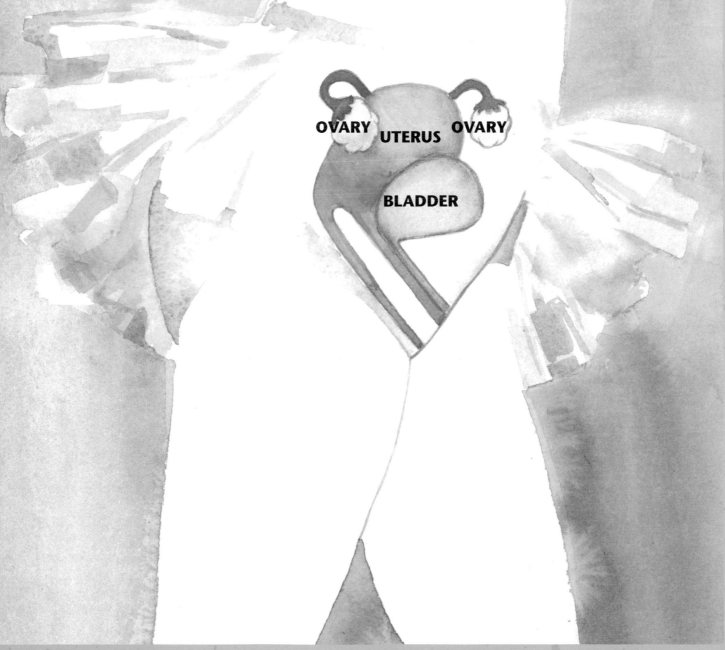

OVARY UTERUS OVARY

BLADDER

Your Hormones and Growing Up

Have you ever seen pictures of yourself as a baby? Can you believe how tiny you were, compared to the big kid you are now? Back then, you couldn't walk, talk, dress and feed yourself, or do a lot of the other stuff you do now. Ever wonder exactly how all this amazing growth took place?

Your *hormones* did it! Hormones are special chemicals made by certain organs, called glands, that are located all throughout your body—like the *pituitary gland* (in your brain), the *thyroid gland* (in your throat), and the *adrenal gland* (in your pancreas), to name a few. Hormones regulate all sorts of processes in your body, including how and when you grow.

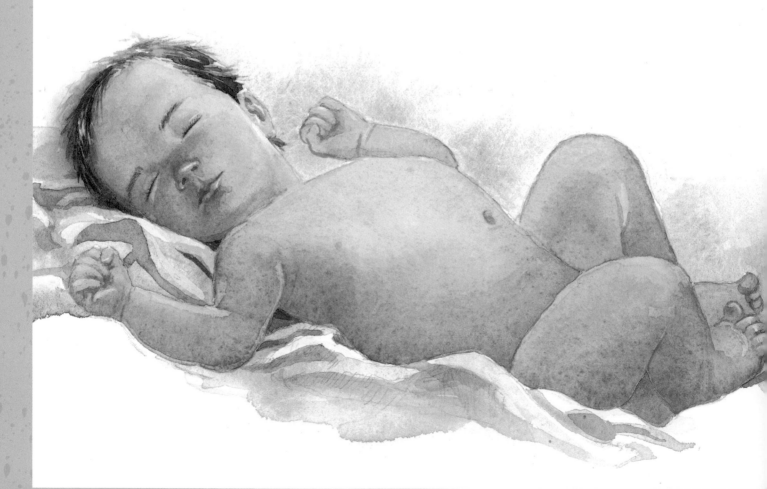

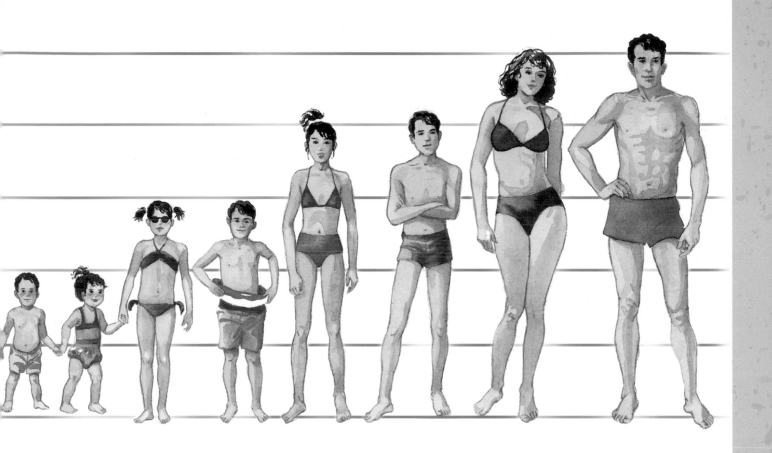

When you were born, you were pretty much helpless. You needed other people to do *everything* for you (including wiping your bottom!). But by the time you were one year old, you had probably learned how to hold a spoon, walk, and say a few words. By the age of two, you had *tripled* your birth weight, you had teeth, could probably talk quite a bit, and were learning rapidly. And by the time you were four, you had reached about 60% of the height you are going to be when you are a grown-up!

Sometime between the ages of 9 and 14, boys and girls go through a growth process called *puberty*. And that's when the hormones really kick in! A boy's voice cracks and gets deeper, his reproductive system matures, and he may even start to grow a mustache. A girl's breasts begin to develop, and her reproductive system matures, too. She will start to lose a little blood through her vagina each month. Don't worry, it's an absolutely normal process! It's called *menstruation*, or "getting a period." By the time a girl is 20 years old, she has pretty much finished growing. A boy, on the other hand, can keep growing until he is 23. (That's why grown-up men are often taller and heavier than grown-up women.)

Now you know all about how *you* work. Aren't you just amazing?

Index